A TRAVEL JOURNAL FOR THE CULTURAL TRAVELER • A TRAVEL JOURNAL

A BICYCLE
TRAVEL JOURNAL

I0088449

Commonwealth Books
an imprint of Applewood Books
Carlisle, Massachusetts

To inquire about this edition
or to request a free copy
of our current catalog
featuring our best-selling books, write to:
Applewood Books
P.O. Box 27
Carlisle, MA 01741
For more complete listings,
visit us on the web at:
www.awb.com

Manufactured in the United States of America

YOUR MOST PERSONAL SOUVENIR

"These empty pages are your future,
soon to become your past.
They will read the most personal tale
you shall ever find in a book."
— ANONYMOUS

The most personal travel keepsake you could ever own is right in your hands. However, just owning this book is not enough, you need to really use it. And, once you do it for one trip, you will want a journal for all of your travels, recording the essence of why you ventured out, how your journey progressed, and the personal memories you might have forgotten if not captured within these pages.

Traveling by bike, whether it is in your native land or somewhere new, in the country or in the city, over mountains or around lakes, provides a uniquely different experience than traveling by foot or motorized vehicle.

"It is by riding a bicycle that you learn the contours
of a country best, since you have to sweat up the
hills and coast down them. Thus you remember
them as they actually are, while in a motor car only
a high hill impresses you, and you have no such
accurate remembrance of country you have driven
through as you gain by riding a bicycle."
— ERNEST HEMINGWAY

Keeping a bicycle travel journal is a deeply personal pursuit. Record all the challenges and accomplishments you think you'll want to remember twenty years from now. That may include the races or tours you have participated in, the places you visited and stayed, the people you encountered, things you found funny, and the sensory memories—smells, sounds, tastes, etc that make your biking trips unique to you. Write about any major milestones, achievements or personal discoveries, and always include the disasters and misadventures—as these will make the best stories to share with others for years to come. Be sure to circle the month and day at the top of each page to help record your timeline.

Throughout this book you will find pages that are blank, with the exception of a quote or two from some from some distinguished cyclists and journal-keepers. These pages are intended to give you the space to draw images that reflect the places, experiences and/or feelings you want to remember, but that can't be captured in a photo. You can also use this space to tape items into your book, such as tickets, postcards, menus, etc.

In order to keep all of your information in one place, you will find helpful pages in the back of the book that provide space for packing lists, helpful bike-travel and repair tips, conversion tables and cycling charts that may come in handy on your journey. There is also a "point page" for those times you find yourself in a place where you do not speak the language, but need to communicate and can do so through universal symbols. Be sure to put your contact information in the back, so if it is lost, a friendly passerby can safely return it to you.

Not every entry has to be brilliant. Writing even small details each day will help you maintain your momentum. Sometimes if you miss writing for a just a couple days, those couple days can quickly become the entire trip—so try to write or record something, no matter how small.

"People who keep journals have life twice."
—JESSAMYN WEST

A BICYCLE TRAVEL JOURNAL

_____

(Destination)

_____

(Dates)

PREPARE

*"Life is like riding a bicycle.
To keep your balance you must keep moving."*
— ALBERT EINSTEIN

Preparation and Anticipation

How did you decide on this destination?

Who has traveled this route before you?

What are some things
you are anticipating about this trip?

What excites you the most?

What makes you nervous?

What do you think the place will be like?

What are things you want to see, smell, and hear?

How have you prepared yourself for this test?

What are the goals you have set for yourself?

Did you buy anything new
especially for this trip?

JAN FEB MAR APR MAY JUN JUL AUG SEP OCT NOV DEC
1 2 3 4 5 6 7 8 9 10 11 12 13 14 15 16 17 18 19 20 21 22 23 24 25 26 27 28 29 30 31

JAN FEB MAR APR MAY JUN JUL AUG SEP OCT NOV DEC

1 2 3 4 5 6 7 8 9 10 11 12 13 14 15 16 17 18 19 20 21 22 23 24 25 26 27 28 29 30 31

JAN FEB MAR APR MAY JUN JUL AUG SEP OCT NOV DEC
1 2 3 4 5 6 7 8 9 10 11 12 13 14 15 16 17 18 19 20 21 22 23 24 25 26 27 28 29 30 31

BON VOYAGE

"Keep a notebook.
Travel with it, eat with it, sleep with it.
Slap into it every stray thought that flutters up into your brain.
Cheap paper is less perishable than gray matter,
and lead pencil markings endure longer than memory."
—JACK LONDON

Travel Companions, Travel Habits, Troubleshooting

Who are your fellow travelers—are there any?

What are three things your travel companion
should know about you?

Have them write down three things
they think you should know about them.

Who do you hope to meet?

Write about your habits
and things you like to bring when traveling.

Have you run into any problems on your journey?
How did you fix them?

Did anything positive come out of this experience,
like meeting someone nice or
learning something new?

JAN FEB MAR APR MAY JUN JUL AUG SEP OCT NOV DEC

1 2 3 4 5 6 7 8 9 10 11 12 13 14 15 16 17 18 19 20 21 22 23 24 25 26 27 28 29 30 31

JAN FEB MAR APR MAY JUN JUL AUG SEP OCT NOV DEC

1 2 3 4 5 6 7 8 9 10 11 12 13 14 15 16 17 18 19 20 21 22 23 24 25 26 27 28 29 30 31

*"Perhaps travel cannot prevent bigotry, but by demonstrating
that all peoples cry, laugh, eat, worry, and die, it can introduce
the idea that if we try and understand each other,
we may even become friends."*
—Maya Angelou

JAN FEB MAR APR MAY JUN JUL AUG SEP OCT NOV DEC
1 2 3 4 5 6 7 8 9 10 11 12 13 14 15 16 17 18 19 20 21 22 23 24 25 26 27 28 29 30 31

JAN FEB MAR APR MAY JUN JUL AUG SEP OCT NOV DEC

1 2 3 4 5 6 7 8 9 10 11 12 13 14 15 16 17 18 19 20 21 22 23 24 25 26 27 28 29 30 31

JAN FEB MAR APR MAY JUN JUL AUG SEP OCT NOV DEC

1 2 3 4 5 6 7 8 9 10 11 12 13 14 15 16 17 18 19 20 21 22 23 24 25 26 27 28 29 30 31

_____

_____

_____

_____

_____

_____

_____

_____

_____

_____

_____

_____

_____

_____

_____

_____

_____

_____

_____

_____

_____

_____

_____

_____

_____

_____

JAN FEB MAR APR MAY JUN JUL AUG SEP OCT NOV DEC
1 2 3 4 5 6 7 8 9 10 11 12 13 14 15 16 17 18 19 20 21 22 23 24 25 26 27 28 29 30 31

EXPLORE

*"One's destination is never a place, but rather
a new way of looking at things."*
— HENRY MILLER

You Have Arrived...

Note the time and write a few sentences about
what you are doing—do this several times
throughout the day.

Use your senses.
What can you see, smell, taste, hear, and feel?

What were the highlights of today?
List five things.

Write about someone you met today.
Recall their appearance, their personality and
mannerisms, the conversation you had with them.
How did they make you feel?

What surprised you the most today?

Look around and observe.
List all the things you see—interactions
between people, people at work or at leisure,
your surroundings, buildings and vehicles,
animals and plants.

What have you done to check that your bike
is in perfect condition?

JAN FEB MAR APR MAY JUN JUL AUG SEP OCT NOV DEC

1 2 3 4 5 6 7 8 9 10 11 12 13 14 15 16 17 18 19 20 21 22 23 24 25 26 27 28 29 30 31

JAN FEB MAR APR MAY JUN JUL AUG SEP OCT NOV DEC

1 2 3 4 5 6 7 8 9 10 11 12 13 14 15 16 17 18 19 20 21 22 23 24 25 26 27 28 29 30 31

"Life is like a ten-speed bicycle.
Most of us have gears we never use."
—CHARLES M. SCHULZ

JAN FEB MAR APR MAY JUN JUL AUG SEP OCT NOV DEC
1 2 3 4 5 6 7 8 9 10 11 12 13 14 15 16 17 18 19 20 21 22 23 24 25 26 27 28 29 30 31

JAN FEB MAR APR MAY JUN JUL AUG SEP OCT NOV DEC

1 2 3 4 5 6 7 8 9 10 11 12 13 14 15 16 17 18 19 20 21 22 23 24 25 26 27 28 29 30 31

JAN FEB MAR APR MAY JUN JUL AUG SEP OCT NOV DEC

1 2 3 4 5 6 7 8 9 10 11 12 13 14 15 16 17 18 19 20 21 22 23 24 25 26 27 28 29 30 31

"I'll tell you what I think of bicycling.
I think it has done more to emancipate women
than any one thing in the world.
I rejoice every time I see a woman ride by on a bike.
It gives her a feeling of self-reliance and independence
the moment she takes her seat; and away she goes,
the picture of untrammeled womanhood."
—SUSAN B. ANTHONY

JAN FEB MAR APR MAY JUN JUL AUG SEP OCT NOV DEC
1 2 3 4 5 6 7 8 9 10 11 12 13 14 15 16 17 18 19 20 21 22 23 24 25 26 27 28 29 30 31

_____

_____

_____

_____

_____

_____

_____

_____

_____

_____

_____

_____

_____

_____

_____

_____

_____

_____

_____

_____

_____

_____

_____

_____

JAN FEB MAR APR MAY JUN JUL AUG SEP OCT NOV DEC

1 2 3 4 5 6 7 8 9 10 11 12 13 14 15 16 17 18 19 20 21 22 23 24 25 26 27 28 29 30 31

JAN FEB MAR APR MAY JUN JUL AUG SEP OCT NOV DEC

1 2 3 4 5 6 7 8 9 10 11 12 13 14 15 16 17 18 19 20 21 22 23 24 25 26 27 28 29 30 31

"Cycle tracks will abound in Utopia."
—H.G. WELLS

JAN FEB MAR APR MAY JUN JUL AUG SEP OCT NOV DEC

1 2 3 4 5 6 7 8 9 10 11 12 13 14 15 16 17 18 19 20 21 22 23 24 25 26 27 28 29 30 31

JAN FEB MAR APR MAY JUN JUL AUG SEP OCT NOV DEC

1 2 3 4 5 6 7 8 9 10 11 12 13 14 15 16 17 18 19 20 21 22 23 24 25 26 27 28 29 30 31

_____

_____

_____

_____

_____

_____

_____

_____

_____

_____

_____

_____

_____

_____

_____

_____

_____

_____

_____

_____

_____

_____

_____

_____

_____

_____

JAN FEB MAR APR MAY JUN JUL AUG SEP OCT NOV DEC

1 2 3 4 5 6 7 8 9 10 11 12 13 14 15 16 17 18 19 20 21 22 23 24 25 26 27 28 29 30 31

JAN FEB MAR APR MAY JUN JUL AUG SEP OCT NOV DEC
1 2 3 4 5 6 7 8 9 10 11 12 13 14 15 16 17 18 19 20 21 22 23 24 25 26 27 28 29 30 31

LIVING THE LIFE

"Ever bike? Now that's something that makes life worth living!...
Oh, to just grip your handlebars and lay down to it,
and go ripping and tearing through streets and road,
over railroad tracks and bridges, threading crowds,
avoiding collisions, at twenty miles or more an hour,
and wondering all the time when you're going to smash up...
And then go home again after three hours of it...
and then to think that tomorrow I can do it all over again!"
— JACK LONDON

Settling In...

Have you developed any
new routines or rituals on your trip?

Draw a map of an area you've gotten to know.
Mark your own landmarks,
like a café where you had a great lunch.

How is your destination different
than you had imagined?

Have you experienced anything
you perceive as a failure?

Write about something that made you
smile or laugh.

Have a travel companion or someone you met
leave you a note or a sketch.

Buy a postcard and send it to yourself back home.
Later you can add this to your journal.

JAN FEB MAR APR MAY JUN JUL AUG SEP OCT NOV DEC

1 2 3 4 5 6 7 8 9 10 11 12 13 14 15 16 17 18 19 20 21 22 23 24 25 26 27 28 29 30 31

_____

_____

_____

_____

_____

_____

_____

_____

_____

_____

_____

_____

_____

_____

_____

_____

_____

_____

_____

_____

_____

_____

_____

JAN FEB MAR APR MAY JUN JUL AUG SEP OCT NOV DEC

1 2 3 4 5 6 7 8 9 10 11 12 13 14 15 16 17 18 19 20 21 22 23 24 25 26 27 28 29 30 31

"A bicycle is a bit like a guitar in that they are both inert objects that only come alive and flourish when put in contact with a human being."
—GARY KEMP OF SPANDEAU BALLET

JAN FEB MAR APR MAY JUN JUL AUG SEP OCT NOV DEC
1 2 3 4 5 6 7 8 9 10 11 12 13 14 15 16 17 18 19 20 21 22 23 24 25 26 27 28 29 30 31

JAN FEB MAR APR MAY JUN JUL AUG SEP OCT NOV DEC

1 2 3 4 5 6 7 8 9 10 11 12 13 14 15 16 17 18 19 20 21 22 23 24 25 26 27 28 29 30 31

JAN FEB MAR APR MAY JUN JUL AUG SEP OCT NOV DEC
1 2 3 4 5 6 7 8 9 10 11 12 13 14 15 16 17 18 19 20 21 22 23 24 25 26 27 28 29 30 31

"When the spirits are low, when the day appears dark,
when work becomes monotonous, when hope hardly seems
worth having, just mount a bicycle and go out for a spin down the
road, without thought on anything but the ride you are taking."
— ARTHUR CONAN DOYLE

JAN FEB MAR APR MAY JUN JUL AUG SEP OCT NOV DEC
1 2 3 4 5 6 7 8 9 10 11 12 13 14 15 16 17 18 19 20 21 22 23 24 25 26 27 28 29 30 31

JAN FEB MAR APR MAY JUN JUL AUG SEP OCT NOV DEC
1 2 3 4 5 6 7 8 9 10 11 12 13 14 15 16 17 18 19 20 21 22 23 24 25 26 27 28 29 30 31

JAN FEB MAR APR MAY JUN JUL AUG SEP OCT NOV DEC

1 2 3 4 5 6 7 8 9 10 11 12 13 14 15 16 17 18 19 20 21 22 23 24 25 26 27 28 29 30 31

"Cycling is possibly the greatest and most pleasurable
form of transport ever invented.
It's like walking only with one-tenth of the effort.
Ride through a city and you can understand its geography
in a way that no motorist, contained by one-way signs
and traffic jams, will ever be able to."
—DANIEL PEMBERTON

JAN FEB MAR APR MAY JUN JUL AUG SEP OCT NOV DEC
1 2 3 4 5 6 7 8 9 10 11 12 13 14 15 16 17 18 19 20 21 22 23 24 25 26 27 28 29 30 31

JAN FEB MAR APR MAY JUN JUL AUG SEP OCT NOV DEC

1 2 3 4 5 6 7 8 9 10 11 12 13 14 15 16 17 18 19 20 21 22 23 24 25 26 27 28 29 30 31

JAN FEB MAR APR MAY JUN JUL AUG SEP OCT NOV DEC

1 2 3 4 5 6 7 8 9 10 11 12 13 14 15 16 17 18 19 20 21 22 23 24 25 26 27 28 29 30 31

JAN FEB MAR APR MAY JUN JUL AUG SEP OCT NOV DEC
1 2 3 4 5 6 7 8 9 10 11 12 13 14 15 16 17 18 19 20 21 22 23 24 25 26 27 28 29 30 31

ADVENTURE

"Get a bicycle. You will not regret it, if you live."
— MARK TWAIN

As You Travel Along…

Will you go higher, farther, faster
than you ever have before?

Choose a different topic each day
to observe and think about.
It could be anything: food, clothes, children,
other tourists, language barriers, transportation

Write about the your three favorite meals
in this place so far. Describe
the restaurant, the food, the people,
and if you tried anything you've never had before.

Did you feel culture shock at any point?
What experiences or events led to this?
Did this event surprise you
or make you uncomfortable? Why or how?

Record any memorable or interesting
quotes from today.

JAN FEB MAR APR MAY JUN JUL AUG SEP OCT NOV DEC

1 2 3 4 5 6 7 8 9 10 11 12 13 14 15 16 17 18 19 20 21 22 23 24 25 26 27 28 29 30 31

_____

_____

_____

_____

_____

_____

_____

_____

_____

_____

_____

_____

_____

_____

_____

_____

_____

_____

_____

_____

_____

_____

_____

_____

_____

JAN FEB MAR APR MAY JUN JUL AUG SEP OCT NOV DEC

1 2 3 4 5 6 7 8 9 10 11 12 13 14 15 16 17 18 19 20 21 22 23 24 25 26 27 28 29 30 31

"I used to work in a bank when I was younger and to me it doesn't matter whether it's raining or the sun is shining or whatever: as long as I'm riding a bike I know I'm the luckiest guy in the world."
— MARK CAVENDISH

JAN FEB MAR APR MAY JUN JUL AUG SEP OCT NOV DEC
1 2 3 4 5 6 7 8 9 10 11 12 13 14 15 16 17 18 19 20 21 22 23 24 25 26 27 28 29 30 31

JAN FEB MAR APR MAY JUN JUL AUG SEP OCT NOV DEC

1 2 3 4 5 6 7 8 9 10 11 12 13 14 15 16 17 18 19 20 21 22 23 24 25 26 27 28 29 30 31

JAN FEB MAR APR MAY JUN JUL AUG SEP OCT NOV DEC

1 2 3 4 5 6 7 8 9 10 11 12 13 14 15 16 17 18 19 20 21 22 23 24 25 26 27 28 29 30 31

"Life is either a daring adventure or nothing."
—HELEN KELLER

JAN FEB MAR APR MAY JUN JUL AUG SEP OCT NOV DEC

1 2 3 4 5 6 7 8 9 10 11 12 13 14 15 16 17 18 19 20 21 22 23 24 25 26 27 28 29 30 31

JAN FEB MAR APR MAY JUN JUL AUG SEP OCT NOV DEC
1 2 3 4 5 6 7 8 9 10 11 12 13 14 15 16 17 18 19 20 21 22 23 24 25 26 27 28 29 30 31

JAN FEB MAR APR MAY JUN JUL AUG SEP OCT NOV DEC
1 2 3 4 5 6 7 8 9 10 11 12 13 14 15 16 17 18 19 20 21 22 23 24 25 26 27 28 29 30 31

"Meet the future; the future mode of transportation
for this weary Western world.
Now I'm not gonna make a lot of
extravagant claims for this little machine.
Sure, it'll change your whole life for the better, but that's all."
— BICYCLE SALESMAN IN
BUTCH CASSIDY AND THE SUNDANCE KID

JAN FEB MAR APR MAY JUN JUL AUG SEP OCT NOV DEC
1 2 3 4 5 6 7 8 9 10 11 12 13 14 15 16 17 18 19 20 21 22 23 24 25 26 27 28 29 30 31

_____

_____

_____

_____

_____

_____

_____

_____

_____

_____

_____

_____

_____

_____

_____

_____

_____

_____

_____

_____

_____

_____

_____

_____

JAN FEB MAR APR MAY JUN JUL AUG SEP OCT NOV DEC

1 2 3 4 5 6 7 8 9 10 11 12 13 14 15 16 17 18 19 20 21 22 23 24 25 26 27 28 29 30 31

_____

_____

_____

_____

_____

_____

_____

_____

_____

_____

_____

_____

_____

_____

_____

_____

_____

_____

_____

_____

_____

_____

_____

_____

JAN FEB MAR APR MAY JUN JUL AUG SEP OCT NOV DEC
1 2 3 4 5 6 7 8 9 10 11 12 13 14 15 16 17 18 19 20 21 22 23 24 25 26 27 28 29 30 31

JAN FEB MAR APR MAY JUN JUL AUG SEP OCT NOV DEC
1 2 3 4 5 6 7 8 9 10 11 12 13 14 15 16 17 18 19 20 21 22 23 24 25 26 27 28 29 30 31

LEARN

"The bicycle is a curious vehicle. Its passenger is its engine."
—JOHN HOWARD

Capturing the Takeaways...

What was the best day or moment on this trip?

How did this trip change your understanding
of this part of the world?

What did you learn about yourself on this trip?

How did your trip make you feel about your bicycle?

What was your biggest
cycling accomplishment of the trip?

If you visited this location again,
what else would you see or do?
What advice would you give to someone
traveling to this place?

How did this trip lead you
to think about your next adventure?

JAN FEB MAR APR MAY JUN JUL AUG SEP OCT NOV DEC

1 2 3 4 5 6 7 8 9 10 11 12 13 14 15 16 17 18 19 20 21 22 23 24 25 26 27 28 29 30 31

JAN FEB MAR APR MAY JUN JUL AUG SEP OCT NOV DEC
1 2 3 4 5 6 7 8 9 10 11 12 13 14 15 16 17 18 19 20 21 22 23 24 25 26 27 28 29 30 31

"When you ride hard on a mountain bike, sometimes you fall—otherwise you're not riding hard."
—GEORGE W. BUSH, FOLLOWING A CRASH INTO A BIKE COP AT THE G8 SUMMIT, GLENEAGLES, SCOTLAND

JAN FEB MAR APR MAY JUN JUL AUG SEP OCT NOV DEC

1 2 3 4 5 6 7 8 9 10 11 12 13 14 15 16 17 18 19 20 21 22 23 24 25 26 27 28 29 30 31

JAN FEB MAR APR MAY JUN JUL AUG SEP OCT NOV DEC

1 2 3 4 5 6 7 8 9 10 11 12 13 14 15 16 17 18 19 20 21 22 23 24 25 26 27 28 29 30 31

JAN FEB MAR APR MAY JUN JUL AUG SEP OCT NOV DEC
1 2 3 4 5 6 7 8 9 10 11 12 13 14 15 16 17 18 19 20 21 22 23 24 25 26 27 28 29 30 31

Ned Flanders: *"You were bicycling two abreast?"*
Homer Simpson: *"I wish. We were bicycling to a lake."*
— THE SIMPSONS, 'DANGEROUS CURVES' EPISODE

JAN FEB MAR APR MAY JUN JUL AUG SEP OCT NOV DEC
1 2 3 4 5 6 7 8 9 10 11 12 13 14 15 16 17 18 19 20 21 22 23 24 25 26 27 28 29 30 31

_____

_____

_____

_____

_____

_____

_____

_____

_____

_____

_____

_____

_____

_____

_____

_____

_____

_____

_____

_____

_____

_____

_____

_____

_____

_____

_____

JAN FEB MAR APR MAY JUN JUL AUG SEP OCT NOV DEC
1 2 3 4 5 6 7 8 9 10 11 12 13 14 15 16 17 18 19 20 21 22 23 24 25 26 27 28 29 30 31

_____

_____

_____

_____

_____

_____

_____

_____

_____

_____

_____

_____

_____

_____

_____

_____

_____

_____

_____

_____

_____

_____

_____

_____

_____

_____

JAN FEB MAR APR MAY JUN JUL AUG SEP OCT NOV DEC

1 2 3 4 5 6 7 8 9 10 11 12 13 14 15 16 17 18 19 20 21 22 23 24 25 26 27 28 29 30 31

"Don't buy upgrades; ride up grades."
— EDDY MERCKX

JAN FEB MAR APR MAY JUN JUL AUG SEP OCT NOV DEC
1 2 3 4 5 6 7 8 9 10 11 12 13 14 15 16 17 18 19 20 21 22 23 24 25 26 27 28 29 30 31

JAN FEB MAR APR MAY JUN JUL AUG SEP OCT NOV DEC

1 2 3 4 5 6 7 8 9 10 11 12 13 14 15 16 17 18 19 20 21 22 23 24 25 26 27 28 29 30 31

JAN FEB MAR APR MAY JUN JUL AUG SEP OCT NOV DEC

1 2 3 4 5 6 7 8 9 10 11 12 13 14 15 16 17 18 19 20 21 22 23 24 25 26 27 28 29 30 31

"Live, travel, adventure, bless, and don't be sorry."
—Jack Kerouac

ORGANIZE

TRIP CHARTS

Date
Location
Distance
Heart Rate
Duration
Altitude
Cadence
Number of Stops
Duration of Stops
Cafe Stops

Date
Location
Distance
Heart Rate
Duration
Altitude
Cadence
Number of Stops
Duration of Stops
Cafe Stops

"Adventure is worthwhile in itself."
— AMELIA EARHART

Date	
Location	
Distance	
Heart Rate	
Duration	
Altitude	
Cadence	
Number of Stops	
Duration of Stops	
Cafe Stops	

Date	
Location	
Distance	
Heart Rate	
Duration	
Altitude	
Cadence	
Number of Stops	
Duration of Stops	
Cafe Stops	

TRIP CHARTS

Date
Location
Distance
Heart Rate
Duration
Altitude
Cadence
Number of Stops
Duration of Stops
Cafe Stops

Date
Location
Distance
Heart Rate
Duration
Altitude
Cadence
Number of Stops
Duration of Stops
Cafe Stops

TRIP CHARTS

Date
Location
Distance
Heart Rate
Duration
Altitude
Cadence
Number of Stops
Duration of Stops
Cafe Stops

Date
Location
Distance
Heart Rate
Duration
Altitude
Cadence
Number of Stops
Duration of Stops
Cafe Stops

TRIP CHARTS

Date
Location
Distance
Heart Rate
Duration
Altitude
Cadence
Number of Stops
Duration of Stops
Cafe Stops

Date
Location
Distance
Heart Rate
Duration
Altitude
Cadence
Number of Stops
Duration of Stops
Cafe Stops

TRIP CHARTS

Date	
Location	
Distance	
Heart Rate	
Duration	
Altitude	
Cadence	
Number of Stops	
Duration of Stops	
Cafe Stops	

Date	
Location	
Distance	
Heart Rate	
Duration	
Altitude	
Cadence	
Number of Stops	
Duration of Stops	
Cafe Stops	

TRIP CHARTS

Date
Location
Distance
Heart Rate
Duration
Altitude
Cadence
Number of Stops
Duration of Stops
Cafe Stops

Date
Location
Distance
Heart Rate
Duration
Altitude
Cadence
Number of Stops
Duration of Stops
Cafe Stops

TRIP CHARTS

Date
Location
Distance
Heart Rate
Duration
Altitude
Cadence
Number of Stops
Duration of Stops
Cafe Stops

Date
Location
Distance
Heart Rate
Duration
Altitude
Cadence
Number of Stops
Duration of Stops
Cafe Stops

FLIGHTS / TRAINS / BUSES / RENTAL CAR
BIKE RENTAL

[#, departure times, confirmation number]

ACCOMMODATIONS / HOTELS

TRAVEL TIPS

1.   Familiarize yourself with your destination before you go by looking at maps and reading about various landmarks. It will all seem more familiar when you get there if you have a head start.

2.   Wake up early and see popular sights before they are crowded with tourists.

3.   Make sure you are covered with inexpensive travel insurance. It can help to replace your more expensive items and protects you against last minute travel cancellations.

4.   Call ahead to hotels and major tourist attractions to see what accommodations they have to keep your bicycle safe and dry.

5.   Get lost on purpose—you'll be surprised at what you might find. (Make sure you have the name and address of your hotel though!)

6.   Avoid long lines at popular attractions by making reservations in advance. Some reservations can even be scheduled and paid for from home before you leave. Just remember to bring all confirmation numbers and printouts with you. Didn't plan ahead? Look for a less-crowded side entrance.

7.   Stay hydrated, eat well, wear sun protection and get enough sleep!

8.   Go where locals go—find off-the-beaten path eateries and activities.

9.   Connect with the concierge at your hotel. They are very knowledgeable and can give you some helpful tips. They even can sometimes order tickets for shows or special exhibits at museums for you, so you can avoid long lines.

10. Research public transportation and museum passes in the cities you are visiting. Often you can get visitor combo passes that can save a lot of money and time. Be sure to find out the rules for bicycles on public transportation in your destination.

11. Call your banks and credit card companies to let them know you're traveling.

EXCHANGE RATES

US DOLLARS	COUNTRY/CURRENCY

METRIC / US CONVERSION CHARTS

CELSIUS	FAHRENHEIT
-10	14
-5	23
0	32
5	41
10	50
15	59
20	68
25	77
30	86
35	95

SPEED	
1 mile per hour (mph)	1.609344 kilometers per hour
1 knot	1.150779448 miles per hour
1 kilometer per hour	0.62137119 mile per hour

LENGTH	
1 inch	= 2.54 centimeters (cm)
1 foot	= 0.3048 meter (m)
1 meter (m)	= 3.280839895 feet
1 kilometer (km)	= 0.62137119 mile
1 mile	= 1.609344 kilometers (km)
1 nautical mile	= 1.852 kilometers (km)

WEIGHT	
1 gram (g)	= 0.001 kilogram (kg)
1 ounce	= 28.34952312 grams (g)
1 pound (lb)	= 16 ounces
1 pound (lb)	= 0.45359237 kilogram (kg)
1 kilogram (kg)	= 35.273962 ounces
1 kilogram (kg)	= 2.20462262 pounds (lb)
1 metric ton	= 1000 kilograms (kg)

VOLUME	
1 US fluid ounce	= 29.57353 milliliters (ml)
1 US cup	= 8 US fluid ounces
1 US pint	= 2 US cups
1 liter (l)	= 33.8140227 US fluid ounces
1 US gallon	= 3.78541178 liters

ADDRESSES
FOR POSTCARDS

_____
Name

_____
Address line 1

_____
Address line 2

_____
City, state, zip, country

_____
Name

_____
Address line 1

_____
Address line 2

_____
City, state, zip, country

_____
Name

_____
Address line 1

_____
Address line 2

_____
City, state, zip, country

ADDRESSES
FOR POSTCARDS

_____

Name

_____

Address line 1

_____

Address line 2

_____

City, state, zip, country

_____

Name

_____

Address line 1

_____

Address line 2

_____

City, state, zip, country

_____

Name

_____

Address line 1

_____

Address line 2

_____

City, state, zip, country

ON THE ROAD BIKE REPAIRS

"Truly, the bicycle is the most influential piece of product design ever."
— HUGH PEARMAN

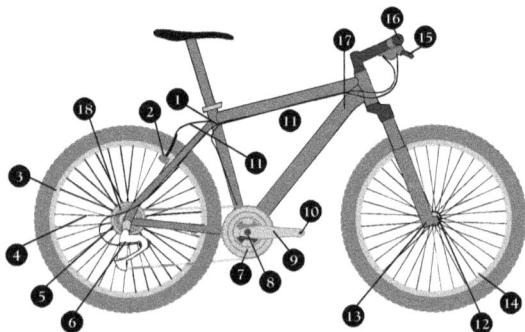

1. BRAKE HOUSING	7. CHAIN RING	13. FRONT DROPOUT
2. BRAKE PADS	8. CRANKSET	14. VALVE STEM
3. RIM	9. CRANK ARM	15. LEVERS
4. SPOKE	10. PEDAL	16. BRAKE HOOD
5. ADJUSTING BARREL	11. BRAKE CABLE	17. CABLE HOUSING
6. REAR DERAILLEUR	12. HUB	18. CASSETTE

FLAT TIRE: Remove wheel from frame and deflate tire. Use tire levers to pry behind the rim. Set the levers about six inches apart and pull the lip of the tire to the outside of the rim. Slide the tire levers away from each other to free the tire from the rim. Remove the tube and either replace it or patch the leak with your patch kit. Reinsert the deflated tube and put the tire back on the bike with the levers.

GEAR NOISE: Clean the chain and chain rings using a rag and degreaser or chain cleaner. Reapply the chain lube to the chain. If noise continues it could need a derailleur adjustment.

SQUEAKY BRAKES: Check brake pads to see if they are worn past the grooves. Replace the pads following directions for installation in the pads kit or by visiting a local bike repair shop. If brakes pads do not need to be replaced try cleaning the wheel and retest. If they are still squeaking the wheel may need balancing.

SHIFTING ISSUES: Clean the cassette of any sticks, grass and mud. Make sure the back wheel is sitting squarely in the dropouts. If the hanger is bent, grab the derailleur with one hand and stick a 5mm hex wrench into the derailleur bolt (the one holding the derailleur on the bike) with the other. Apply pressure to both the derailleur and wrench to get the hanger as close to straight as possible. Shift the gears to test. Turn the barrel adjuster (knob on the shift cable) either in or out to center the derailleur over the cog with each shift to eliminate jumping. Check derailleur stops in the highest and lowest gears to prevent the chain from jumping off the cassette. Check the cables and replace if needed.

BROKEN SPOKE: Spokes break from fatigue. As the wheel goes around, the spokes change tension and they'll gradually fatigue and break. You're more likely to break a spoke if you have a heavy load, your wheels have few spokes, and you travel long distances. If it's broken at the elbow, you can undo the spoke nipple and just pull it out. If it's broken at the threads, unthread it from the hub. You can do this if there aren't any disc rotors or rear cassettes in the way. If there are, twist it around a neighboring spoke or tie it in place to keep it out of the way until you get home. With a new spoke, thread it through the hub—notice if it should be head out or head in. Cross the new spoke over and under the other spokes (matching the pattern of the rest of the wheel) to reach the vacant spoke hole in the rim, lube the spoke thread and thread a spoke nipple on to the end. Stick the wheel in a truing jig or back in the bike and tighten the new spoke so it's the same tension as all the others.

PACKING TIPS

1. Don't forget your passport and a back up photo ID, such as a driver's license or state ID. Make photocopies of these documents, leaving one at home and bringing one with you.

2. If possible, bring more than one credit card and ATM card. That way, if one has a problem, you have a backup. Before you leave, see if your bank has a partnership with another bank where you are traveling. You may not be charged ATM fees with the partnering bank. Also, many automated machines overseas only accept credit cards with computer chips in them.

3. Be sure to share your itinerary with someone at home, so they know how to reach you if needed.

4. Check your phone plan before you go to make sure it can be used internationally. Many phone plans cannot be used overseas, and you may need to buy a temporary plan or rent an international cell phone for the time period you are away. This can take time to set up, so plan ahead.

5. If you're bringing a tablet or smart phone, back up your devices before you leave. You'll be glad if they are lost or stolen.

6. Bring an adapter and international plug converters for electronics.

7. Pack light. If you're questioning whether or not to bring something, you don't really need it. Be sure to check the airlines extra fees for checking bikes to avoid being surprised at the airport!

8. Check all airport restrictions and guidelines. All liquids packed in your carry-on must be in containers no bigger than 3 oz and all have to fit in a 1-quart ziplock bag (combined), and wear easily removable shoes, and don't wear a belt in order to get through security faster.

PACKING LIST

FOR YOUR TRIP:

Bike

Helmet

Cycling jersey and padded shorts

Gloves

Rainwear

Sunglasses/Eye protection

Hydration pack

Saddlebag

Handlebar bag

Cargo rack and trunk bag

Headlight

Taillight

Bike lock

Cell phone/GPS/charger

Sunscreen

Bungee cords

Plastic baggies to keep items dry

Toilet paper or moist towelettes

Rubber sink plug to wash clothes
    in the sink

Bug spray

Diaper rash cream or bag balm
    (heals any saddle sores)

Steel-reinforced epoxy putty
    (like JBWeld SteelStik) for
    on-the-go repairs

Spare spokes (min of 6)

Spoke wrench

Add extra empty lines

Lubricant

Brake and derailleur cables

Spare cleats

Duct tape

YOUR DAILY BIKE BAG:

Always wear your ID bracelet
    with emergency contact info,
    name and blood type.

Camera/Cell phone

Cash/credit card

Spare tube

Pump

Tire levers

Spare chain links/chain tool

Cycling multi-tool
    w/Allen wrench

Tire iron

Patch kit

Small Phillips head screwdriver
    and hex keys

Pressure gauge

CO2 cartridge

First Aid Kit

Small towel

Bug spray

Lip balm

Sunscreen

Hydration and food items

*Of course, don't forget the
other essentials such as under-
wear, clothing, toiletries and
shoes other than your cleats!

POINT PAGE

Symbol	Translation	Symbol	Translation

If this journal is found,
please be so kind to return it to:

_____
Name

_____
Address line 1

_____
Address line 2

_____
City, state, zip, country

_____
Email address

_____
Phone

Emergency contacts

_____
Name

_____
Email address

_____
Phone

_____
Name

_____
Email address

_____
Phone

www.ingramcontent.com/pod-product-compliance
Lightning Source LLC
Chambersburg PA
CBHW040207060426
42445CB00036B/1967